The Light Breaks Open

Also by Sarah Tiffen and published by Ginninderra Press
Learning Country
Mythica

Sarah Tiffen

The Light Breaks Open
Tales of a different dreaming

The Light Breaks Open: Tales of a different dreaming
ISBN 978 1 74027 495 1
Copyright © Sarah Tiffen 2008

First published 2008
Reprinted 2019

GINNINDERRA PRESS
PO Box 3461 Port Adelaide 5015
www.ginninderrapress.com.au

Contents

The Light Breaks Open	9
Australia Day	10
Condobolin Haiku	14
Temporality	16
To the Blood and Honey	17
Rain Shadow	20
The Outsiders	21
Farmer's Wife	24
The Bush is an Animal	25
Farm at Dusk I	26
Farm at Dusk II	27
The Day Before the Wedding	29
Two Worlds	35
Rain Event in the Whispering Country	36
My Sad Country (*Drought Cycle I*)	40
On the Plains (*Drought Cycle II*)	42
The Big Brown (*Drought Cycle III*)	43
Bushfire (*Drought Cycle IV*)	47
Communion: The Dreaming Tree	48
Prehistorica *Birds and Dogs*	53
Convincing Ground	56
The Divine Mundane	57

For Tom, Lil and Wilbur

For my friends, who have been there from before the start

Thank you for keeping me alive

You and I will fold the sheets...
Your turn. Now mine.
We fold them and put them away until they are needed...
A wish for all people when they lie down to sleep –
Smooth linen, cool cotton, the fragrance and stir of herbs
And the faint but perceptible scent of sweet clear water
           Rosemary Dobson

'With all its sham, drudgery and broken dreams it is still a beautiful world. Be cheerful. Strive to be happy.'
           Desiderata

The Light Breaks Open

The crooked hills – earth's grave pelvis –
cradle crook the cocooned day
cupped in the crescent
iliac-crested kernelling
all that promised future
borne in bone
the sky blue calcium of shell trembling
membrane, fragile nested egg of soon
then –
the Light breaks open, spilled from the
hills' hip, deeply held – released,
intimate,
incandescent –
day, life, hope.

Australia Day

The sun rose early, an egg cracked open.
Shearing before breakfast.
Men and boys in shorts and dusty boots
moved amongst brackish shade in the distance,
bracken-dappled, coolish-breeze soughing.

Light like an old photograph spilled
down the runs, out of the shearing sheds'
corrugated iron and ironbark.
Border collie barks, and sheep,
pink, naked and spindly,
ran dispersing like bubbles in a stream.

*

Sounds rose upward with heating air
across the farm's amphitheatre.
The quiet land paused.
Like soloists each sheep uttered the guttural ovine 'maaahh'.
Cockatoos scratched tin on glass, and
crows scraped a rusted iron hinge,
atonal, cynical, resigned.
And then the galahs flurry – the net of tiny shards
shook and shook through trees
flicker their chaotic strobing semaphore –
grey, pink, grey, pink.
Further off the throaty moan of autumn drop bulls,
mounting each other in their bullish eagerness.

*

Feeding out at ten, the dusty ute pitching and rattling
under bales the size of outhouses.
Cattle mooned in, laconic, unflappable and sleek,
bred to a shiny placidity. The muscle under their black hides
jostled the taught membranes
like black velvet sacks crammed with dogs.
The paddocks released vapours like petrol fumes
and dust-stirred willy-willies, like red smoke stacks
from underground caverns, were dervishes whirling the topsoil to
   the sea.
A sapphire sky washed in the sophist sun's gold milk.

*

The day became burning bronze.
In Forbes the grand architecture of the post office, the bank,
and the guilded pubs sat glistening in heat.
A P-plater, her Holden adorned in twitching Aussie flags, did laps
while Advance Australia Fair trailed from her window
like a single strand of tinsel, tinny, old-world.
Outside the Vandenberg Hotel,
black children played dinks, twirling and circling
on their makeshift bikes, smiling gleefully and
calling 'g'day' to passers-by, testing the mood of
solidarity and nationalism, relishing the holiday.
Up the street, on a bench outside the Wattle Café,
two white boys, callow and small-eyed, muttered
'little niggers', then called it down the emptiness.
Backyards were full of people quietly getting pissed.

*

Leaving the cool of the RSL, the heat was like a wall
that you hit. The riverbank was lined with utes
pulled right up to the edge of the Lachlan by
blue tarps pulled between trees on ropes:
these installations of 'long-weekend'–
take a slab and the fishing rods, wife, mates, kids –
and sit in the still air and the silver curtains of insect noise
waiting by the brown water for fish to bite, watching for snakes
to not.
The landscape a hypnotist.

*

Afternoon flattened to uniform thickness
and the air like a hot flannel.
Everything slowed – trees moved barely in dense syrup
and the clock paused, too tired to go on.
Animals dispersed to shade and posed in stances of
lying, crouching, languishing – outcrops
of ornamental sculpture, waiting out the heat.
Sleep came like a coma washed over by a whirring of fan blades.
In a breathy magic, white curtains moved like seaweeds
while the air pressed in.

*

Then later, early evening – more work, fencing and
feeding the cattle again. Shadows lengthened, and the horizon
hurtled gold. Birds grew restless and swung
choreographed across the midfield, releasing their
high pitch of evening sound, a scatter of glass pebbles into
golden brassy air.

Animals walked across moving paddocks, against the tide
of shadows, stalking on shadow stilts, scolding the seeping dark.
The horizon now a jewelled furnace, now a mauve requiem,
then finally the palest green – a gauze shift wrapped on the thin
blade of the shoulder of the ranges, sprinkled with pale diamantes.
The lady evening passes delicately.
Night is black velvet.

*

Beers, under the air conditioner. Braving the mozzies
to see the comet cut its mystic way across the western sky
lit up by a million stars. Breathtaking, massive, infinite.
Wrapped in cool sheets, the heat still palpable from the floor,
sleep came again near midnight…
later still, the wind picked up in the forest beyond the river,
roaring and soulful in the watchful dark and the
land like a great spirit shifted and rumbled as a cool change
spiked the night.

Feet touching, and the barest touch of fingertips –
love's dark mystery, even in sleep.
The white noise of eucalypt-channelling winds, the scent of dung,
and the feel of something unknown yet familiar.

Australia Day.

Condobolin Haiku

Land like parchment
written in ancient rock scapes
heiroglyphics shift redly in late light.

*

Road as straight as a post
carves through blood country.
Earth parts and yields as we drive.

*

The low porch houses giant pine stumps.
The herb garden amass with weed.
Cold evening glows with firelight.

*

Cows, patient as nurses,
butt and low outside the window.
Rain hushes – the roof sunk with fallen cloud.

*

Red rock looming.
'Sacred place,' they say.
Shadows in the contours.

*

Red-gum sleepers, blood-coloured.
Hewn strangely to thick lengths,
pieces of forest – violence in their symmetry.

*

Sawdust like grated carrot, mountains of it.
Chiselled to reveal the hewn sleeper, blood colour.
The forest is torn and massacred.

Temporality

The clock treads its inexorable steps,
as the house floods momentarily
with the hot gold of the first light.
Branches instructed by winds
move soundlessly behind the curtain
silhouetted for momentary shadow play.
A perfect shadow of a bird alights, bobs, flees.
The moment looms large and silent
resisting the tidal flow of the second hand
tick-tick-tick.
Ever briefly, it holds its own poise
a slight hesitation, the current
slightly arrested, slightly…slightly…
A moment borrowed from infinity,
out of time
for the heart weighed down by blood,
by its own beat.

To the Blood and Honey

We drove out through the tin hills all blue and wrinkled in the light,
and somehow the country absorbed us as we drove, and spoke until we were
only one with that place, and spirits rose out of the red earth there
infused with the radiance of sun
diffused through blood and tears.

The country there grew older by degree as we moved north, with its own majestic flatness
and then taking on the ancient strangeness of rock and uncleared eucalypt and the wild country gathering in
in bulbs of red rock, monoliths and folds of earth and clusters, saturated with the blood deep down.
From these, streams of light spilled redly and shadows fingered the rich bunched earth, scrub and stubble,
and from outcrops of hidden caverns and jutting edges,
a sense of Olgas, and of God
and we pushed on into the rust-coloured whispering country,
and it was outside my understanding of country
and travelling to a new, foreign and heartfelt land,
to the rose-coloured blood and honey land.
And the colour, the colour of that earth, that red red of ancient rust,
leached upward through grasses, trunks and branches, through foliage
and into the very sky
so that everything, the whole landscape and magic world
was tinged with the blood colour.

I felt the trembling of the spirits in that ancient soil
and they entered me and
I was hungry for it.

*

We walked in through the crouching forest, all dappled and ghostly
   in the striped light,
stripped back and perspectiveless, the tangle of pink and white and
   olive gave
tapestry sense, glassy submergence in a light cave of peppered
   limestone,
and the scent of eucalyptus, fresh and strange rose about us, and the
   forest creaked and
bled, starkly folded back to show the blistered jewels,
the knobs of giant sap glass frank upon the weeping weighty bodies
   of the river gums.
The land was ancient, even its measured paddocks, and its stock
   routes and
timber-felling industries, and anomalies of Harbour Bridge
   remnants, and channels,
and breeding sheds, such trappings and modernities.
Beneath the land was a vast crouching thing, older than the oldest
   tree – bestial, patient,
and the red colour murmuring under all.
Beneath the light
the spirits whispered to us low and loudly, pushing and swishing,
   and shimmering
in the glistening treetops, and moving swiftly and slowly telling
their stories to our hearts.
Mighty land of blood and honey. Mighty forest roaring in the dark.
   Mighty river labouring below.
The sense of might was fearful strange and wonderful; we tried
to comprehend the darkness of this whispering country,
we held each other divining the power from
the motherlode of earth.

*

We felt the magnitude of it, paddocks that stretched and stretched
    out beyond territories,
swaths of land and grasses whispering language to us that we could
    not quite fathom, then felt in our
bodies and bone and made the song to each other with our skin and
    eyes and fingertips.
The light was a plangent blue, frank with heat, and through it the
    river reds dissolved in liquid,
in the peppered oily sheen and I waited to feel the clear seams of
    language in the rock
from blood and honey built, and some kind of menace hovered, a
    kind of fear
crept out of the seeping red land into us…
and I submitted to the land when we
felt it uttering us and issuing us forth
I reached out for the language of the blood and honey, and reached
    in to landscapes of
rough terrain, the haunted heart interior.
And the language before language is the clicking rhythms of bark
    and stick and
dust and creaking dappled tree – I wanted to belong with words but
could only walk and watch and wait.

It is only through initiation,
scarred and hardened, that the mighty land
with its secret poetry,
would take us in to that
wide flat song of flesh made one.

Rain Shadow

It is hard to stay hopeful
when the season has been so harsh,
when the tendrils of green curling joy
are burnt beneath the cruel glare of a damaged heat
and the juice of sweet love, flowing with the future,
fight dry beneath a bleak sun of doubt.

The happy shining wilts
battling against a fierce glare of dark possibilities.
It is too hot for gentle tender touch.
Lips parch and peel, thirsty for the water of each other,
and find the brown mirage of self-doubt's deception.

The heart is laden with heat
and hope turns to anxious fear…
Love in a time of drought.

It is hard to believe,
when promised rain evaporates high in the stratosphere,
and the birds are panting on the brown lawn, incongruous
and strange. All is a world of strangeness, and
underneath arrhythmia of a heart in peril,
depleted and dehydrated,
longing for the river of joy to break its banks
and wash the hungry fear away.

Fingers tremble, the bed of soft green
dries up to a flinty grey.
Dust chokes words of faith
and prayers for resilience.
The bond must be deep-rooted, seeking
moisture from deep underground,
must be hardy, and dogged to survive…
Love in a time of drought.

The Outsiders

This is the whispering country.
It is not ours.
Though we have spread ourselves upon it,
tried to harness and chart it
it does not bend to us.
This is the heart of the heartland,
the place where we journey in.
But the further we press on her ravaged flanks
the more lost we become,
until we see this is foreign country.
It is foreign or else it is we.
This is the whispering country.

Spirits chastise and watch us at every turn,
though we have ignored them.
We have moved about as masters.
We have lorded and fenced, emptied and demarcated.
We have built gardens, stud yards, empires.
We have dug and scarred.

We have even moved about in great love,
coming to graft ourselves upon the country,
turning hybrid.
We have soaked enough topsoil in through the
membranes of our lungs and eyes, now
coursing the ventricles of our subconscious
to have the land within us.
We have stood about in wonder, hats cocked,
and finally seen the beauty in the
motherfolds of red rock and
the cathedrals of trees.

Even the fierce sky has moved us.
But it is not our place.
It is not ours.

This is the whispering country.
The pines we planted ache and groan with the
weight of the century.
We came from highlands and dales, marvelling at space
and mystery.
We brought animals to fill the emptiness.
We heard silences, fretted, and prospered.
We misunderstood even as we conquered.

No words of ours can describe it,
and those whose could we silenced.
We made profit castles from dirt and gold.
We let cyanide seep to the river.
We gloated and dug at the hills,
thinking to explain them to ourselves,
but no language we command could
articulate the fear,
the archaic majesty,
the shame and darkness,
the shifting perspectiveless light.

The whispering builds to a howling,
the jutted rock lives with its figures and secrets.
We can't see them, and will not be privy
though they watch us.

We can scar ourselves upon it, and
score it across our chests,
we can wait to belong to it,
we can even lie beneath it.

The land we try to love…

but we are always the outsiders.

Farmer's Wife

In the early times, it was hopeful,
much more than a gesture…purposeful –
to step to the veranda to look skyward
for signs of cloud…

Weeks turned to dust.
Months turned to dying stock.
The years inscribed their toll upon her face,
at the brow, the pinched lips, the
waiting in her eyes…

Eventually it became a ritual,
and compulsion.
The daily tread to the sky's edge,
like a beseeching wordless prayer:
after breakfast,
to wipe her hands on the worn tea towel,
untie her apron and hang it on the kitchen chair,
then push the screen door slowly, and step out
onto worn boards, step right to the lip of the
old veranda, and push her hair from her eyes,
raise her arm across her brow,
and squint out into the light.
Brighter than a blade
waterless and fierce,
and that cruel, cruel blue…
Now she thinks in her darker moments
if she doesn't look, the rain will steal away
to where another more worthy supplicant is waiting.

She tries not to let her thoughts
get too loud.

The Bush is an Animal

Like an animal, it crouches,
makes shadow, creaking and groaning.
A snap, and a wind-rushing roar
and a dark maul and a beat.
It rises and urges.
Lie still before it rigid with fear
breath behind the ear and out of sight.
Creature, presence, spirit, wild.
The bush beyond the river, growling.

Farm at Dusk I

To find the essence of this place,
stand in a dry paddock at the close of day
amidst oceans of grain whispering their blue sheen
with the sun draining the day off the rim of the world.
Everything streams west.
Fingers of shadow strain eastward clutching the light.
The curvature of trees along the river gather in shadows to roost.
Gauze clouds of dust form a halo.
Cattle nudge and snort at the fence line,
stranded in fading light.
A man in silhouette against the orange sunset –
there is only the earth and sky…
and animals conducting their rituals.
The land is flat and massive.
The sky is a darkening canvas.
After sunfall, time stops
as the ground air cools and the
insects rise in their columns of sound,
then night descends, black as tar,
total dark, but for stars in their millions above.

Later the moon rises as a third coming –
vast over the forest.
Before it crowns, the light burns below the hills –
men suspect bushfire, or armageddon.
After, the landscape is blue and luminous, the bush a perfect mystery,
whilst crickets augment the vast silence,
the land like a presence, envelops.

Our country.

Farm at Dusk II

The land mass, like a great parched blotting sheet,
draws off all colour at the close of day:

off the sky's magnificence and birds' wings, and backs of cattle,
off light beam treetops that shimmered in midday glare,
then lengthening through afternoon when sheep graze
in lucerne and are lit up orangely, the swathes of coloured paddock
in reds and bleached gold applied on the days' vast canvas, and
   chance greens of barley.
The land like a sponge soaks it down,
draws it away, as evening comes.

Then the river in its deep sedentary bed – the lowest point in all the
   miles,
becomes a seam of darkest green
the light conduit, the thief of day, draining the
light away.
Absorbs all light down into its own darkening
deeper below the gullied banks
trees flanking replicate,
concentrating the fluctuates of colour into their consecrate shadows.
The sky relinquishes itself,
shedding down to the palest blush –
like a shyly bared buttock, pale and vulnerable –
and the land, and the river,
form down, down that deepening portal drawing all down
through the seam.

Somewhere below all this, light and day
are harboured in the mystical subterranean cavern,
blinding in its concentrate.

*

On the Lachlan's blown-glass surface, a duck commands an
    arrowhead of water shape.
One snag archly curved refracts itself in
the river's immovable sheen.
River gums leviathan, and gathered in memoriam,
with huge girth
they yawn up, lean in, fingering the river,
poised for mercy, mourning, confidential,
other-worldly: river red gums
bear witness and shield the river
with patrician calm…

Like a rare cloth the day slips from the lacquered surface of the world
Down to the subterranean vault,
to the dark velvet secret of the river's deeps,
the silent chasm.
Evening settles like a flung sheet.
The smells of green stalks and dung emit from the cool,
make passage for the mysterious dark and the intimate lunar odour
    of the night.

Like a requiem, the heartbreak of sheep's 'mawww'
wavering on rising wind.

The Day Before the Wedding

The day before the wedding
the moon stayed in the sky till late, as big as a beacon,
a benevolent eye, shedding its lunar sheen,
even as the sun hung nigh.

The dawn before was that satin event, though still,
like a painting of satin, shot with greens and seeping rose –
cool delicate hues, innocent of the hot promise of the day.
Birds sang stilly, held in the tension between waning moon
and rising sun, which moved inexorably across the paddocks' pearly
   sway,
the light shimmering off the cattle run
the day before the wedding.

Defying the horizon, the sun in its coming was declarative
and bright. Every clod and blade bestowed with its own discrete shadow
and the scrubby olive hills lit up as though gold were spilt.
The bush in its scribbled mystery gave off a moist pepper smell,
and morning birds fell upward numerously on their grazing flight,
   up to the sky's hilt.

At the farm, they lay, and the paddocks spread before them
muted and murmuring the colour of doves.
As the light swung and changed it seemed water lapped round, the
old farmhouse an island fortress, built only on their whispered loves.

On rising currents off the land, more scents –
the familiar brown of sod, a faint green smell of crop
newly wet by scant rain, an undertone of sheep
and dog –
these farming smells, that had accompanied them since
childhood, of animal and soil,

that had been the backdrop to their meeting,
to their moving inward to the source, and to their
loving: sweet earthy smell, the perfect foil.

With the warming of the morning,
light moved in lattices across the window and laced the bed.
She took his calloused hand above the blankets
and held it to her lips, and he, pulling his mind from the cloudless
sky bent to smell her apple smell and felt the soft curvature of her hips,
that mirrored the curve of the earth on the far horizon of that flat
lapping country. It was all in the look; and nothing but sweet
   nothing said.

From the corner of his eye, close up, he saw the freckles on her nose,
familiar, sweet and comforting, his home country,
and breathing her, felt the deep sounder of the earth booming up,
the spirit level finding its equilibrium, on this day,
this sweet day, hot and blinding and rainless, then some rag cloud,
and light dust, and lowing cattle and the lonely sheep sound,
the day before the wedding.

After breakfast, he drove north in the old ute,
trundling the gravel roads to his father's farm, his arm aslant the
   window frame, as
he surveyed the passing land, ageless and mute,
while she made the journey of ages,
locked arms with her bridesmaids, the ritual
as they understood, and whispered and
laughed and drove round the district,
phone calls, waxing, filing nails and painting,
listening to wise old women's counsel,
taking her last steps toward womanhood.

As he rode the motorbike up and down furrows, squinting into the sun,
like a boy in a boat bobbing through the bays, and mustered the sheep
for market, he saw the sky as a great empty sea, and thought tomorrow
the sailing ship of his marriage would launch upon it, and they would
make their own waves and ways,
and he saw a lone eagle
linocut across his sight line, sharp and soaring as a scalpel,
creature of dreams, marking the scudding cloud displays.
And felt the magnitude of his feat, to live and breath,
to work the soil, and then, to woo this woman to his side,
his wife-to-be, his bride.

As he contemplated this beneath mirageous sky,
she moved in a darting choreography, from florist, to salon,
phoned her mother, absorbed the smiles and prayers
of all women who saw her and blessed her with their
glistening eyes, and old women who patted her hand and
said, 'her grandmother would be proud', and she would make
a beautiful bride. 'Good girl', they said and she
glowed with their secret hope and pride, and they saw in her
the girls they had been, and all the joys of their
beginnings, before the ravages of time and tide.

She glowed inwardly and outwardly, the girl-woman,
flowering through that day in to the bride she was born to be.
And thoughts of longing filled her for the strong darling that was
   husband, he.

As he loaded sheep on the truck, and drove the long miles
to the sales, she was dreaming and talking of flowers, and shoes,
diamonds and veils.

Then she drove too, through the paddocks of her childhood, wide
  and bright, to
her father's house, and drank tea with the mob, and turned the
pages of the old photo album laughing at the kid in jeans
swinging wide to the sky, and her brothers came in from
the long stride across paddocks taut with drought, and laughed, and
tackled her and tickled her while she squealed, and Mother came to
  rouse,
and the dry light streamed upward from the cracked earth,
and the smell of dust and tea, and grease and blundstones,
and lavender, and her mother's cooking – the warmth circling her
  since birth.

The day before the wedding, so much toing and froing, so much
  froth, and bother,
the tears and the waft of perfume in the garden. Over cold beer,
the men assented, nodding: 'best to stay out of the way'. So they
  drove about,
tinkering with gates and wire, checked the crops, and stood to cock
  their hats and shake their heads at the
sky's rainless haze; this the three-hundredth day.
Out on the long roads, cars, passing one another, pulled over, and folk
got out to yarn, and speculate – the weather, price of lambs
going down, and the impending nuptials, the chance of rain,
'Buckley's and none', they chuckled, voices gravel-pitched – and added,
'fancy that little girl and the big fella, gettin' hitched.'
All the district knew them – and willed them toward this coming union,
and the shared joy of 'girl meets, loves and marries boy'.
Rain or no, their day already made.

While she tried her dress on for the last time, in bare feet on the carpet
of her mother's room, and the women gathered round whispering, and
fingered the satiny white, and wept and patted her, and she wept too,
perceiving fully, that things would change tomorrow,
shifting like cloud mass moving its shadow over afternoon
    paddocks,
and that she was on the threshold, and her golden moment come,
it all came upon her as she stood there, the day before her marriage
    rite…

He, in his work clothes, and covered in sheep dust, did the rounds
of the farm to compose himself, penned sheep, penning poetry in
    his head,
called the dog to him, watching the sun shift westward, the last sunset
of his youth, his onlyness, he too so well aware, of his pledge, of stepping
up to the call of his heart and fate, and the thought of her face, his
    heart's balm
and his truth.

And so on in to the wedding eve, and people gathering from work
    and the business of the day,
the flock called in beneath the steeple of the small red-brick church,
for the big rehearsal, and twilight filtered through the darkling air,
in webbed visions of dream, and boys and girls,
flushed with the flurry of their labours and excitement, face-to-face,
    and bright-eyed, came
like actors to the stage – the wedding party to rehearse the ancient
    ritual,
how to be and move and speak, each part to play…

And she, barefoot in jeans, on her father's arm (he in his work clothes,
abashed and proud, and teary-eyed,) walked down the aisle.
The groom-to-be confronted by the sight of his young nearly-wife
looking as sweet and unadorned and game as any farmer's daughter
    could –
he stood by the altar and wiped his eyes, and looked as though he
    never
was so proud, the look of love, the awkwardness, the blush of
    gratitude…
as they together stumbled through their practice vows, that
    hallowed eve,
before the old familiar crowd, the love, the future, hovering in view,
and sweetly kissed and lately wise,
the covenant was early sealed, as consecrate as any service or
formality, say she, say he, forever be, I'm thine and thee for me,
for all eternity.

The day before the wedding.

Two Worlds

In town, groups of women and children
arrange themselves by seats, and against the
plate glass of shopfronts,
hanging around cars and
scattering in gutters, doorways.
Young men join them.
The dark skin is a foreignness,
though they are more home than any.
The light flings off the street like striking tin.

Coloured shirts stand out – red, white,
black, yellow. The little ones stare.
Then they are laughing.
They kick the ground, curse, embrace each other.
They are from somewhere far away,
which is here.

White women, thin as posts and emu-like
turn their heads a little, eyes averted,
mouths tight from years of flies,
and dust, the currency of the held tongue,
the flies. The struggle with them.

The pursed lips hold back the words –
from the century past – the shock,
the fear, the companionship and yes, distaste – and
late at night, the shame,
the strangled sorry,
in between breaths.

Rain Event in the Whispering Country

I

The black cattle congregate to blink at grapefruit splendour,
that gold satellite hanging over them.
Incomprehensible.
The moon – woman-steeped, bringer of blood, the mother cycle –
which rose from the land line late and fast
bringing a low tide of warmth.
Vast rose-coloured, milky petal-textured, pot of
clotted cream. Her rich tangerine fullness, like a swollen areola
in the full breast of that night.
She leaked her salty hind milk down
spilling out on the brooding cattle country,
on sweet-faced Angus, and
filling the Lachlan languid through dark floodplain.
The whole flat whispering country
bathed in the mystery blue,
salt-licked by the syrup of milky lume.
Before the rain,
the world in dilation, swelling.
Later, a rainbow ringed the moon high up –
'this means rain,' he said.

II

We woke before dawn
to the never-forgetting sound on the high tin roof,
the heart-settling roar and
the sight from the homestead window framed in white voile, of a
world corrugated with falling sheets of tin-coloured water,
the vague mist, the warmth, the matched rising in our bodies, and
our hearts, long drought-stricken, drinking up.

The rain rose like a crowd
calling itself joyously,
All day the chain mail of rain riding the low horizon,
grass battened and anointed in a burnished brass, and green
   relishing itself
newly-discovered in the downed shields of glassy puddles
throwing back anodised sky. The looming.
In the heavy, sodden light, the mirrored earth, glazed copper-minted soil
thickening and sighing.
Evening winged in.
It fell in smokey curtains of cloud,
the land pressed lavishly by the spun velvet of
blue upon grey upon darker blue and purple,
horizons of indigo shades backing onto themselves,
fold after fold of the thick, mohair light,
mauve and darkling, close and pregnant with knitted moisture.
Cattle walked upside down in sunk heavens, through
the magic country wrapped in the soft valedictory rain,
and its beautiful cloud breath, dark and huddled.
Rain, rain, rain – all day they talked of it, calmed, jubilant,
   breathing ozone
those townsfolk, whom I moved amongst thinking
of love and God.
Rain's slaking mystery.
The ancient land lay in submission.
The stationary yellow river began moving quickly,
secretly swollen.

III

After the rain
the contraction, the sharpening and tightening.
The land pulled in, soaking the water into itself,
drinking, hoarding.
The moon shook foil over the crouching land,
silver sheets of tinny silverly crackling stuff
pressed down round the hills and ridges sculpturally.
The ancient soughing place took on the surreal artifice of built things,
sharp lunar light made a foil Christo effect the barely undulating
    paddocks,
all silvery-blue and coated.
Round and shiny, like a milk-bottle lid,
the pinned two-dimensional moon, incandescent, small and hard
against the night's felt board,
channelled the brittle frosted light from beyond the universe's
darkest holy blue.

The air in our throats cold hard and silver, arctic.

Beneath the iron winter of that night the land contracted,
hardening, crouching down, turning in.
Beneath sharpness, the earth rumbled and churned, digesting rain.
Worms and roots traversed it.
The cold was from the earth's bowels,
sepulchral, acid, stripped us clear, and left us as figures
made of light in the cold shoulder
of the farm.
From this stark beauty
we turned in, curled to a kernel together.

Through crystalline air, the sound of cattle
butting and lowing in the garden,
the sweet animal smell of their hot breath.
Vapours.

My Sad Country (*Drought Cycle I*)

O my sad country
you have laid down to the heat
you are bent beneath the weight of waterless skies
the air is a forest of grass sound, insect scrapings, paper rustling
the sheets of rasping, the scratching of bird cries
against the glass surface of the day.

O my sad country
you are built for sadness
your brown river moves in languid melancholy silence
through eucalypt forest always a study of lingering grief
glistening slowly in the oily light. Cicadas' still-silver sheen pulses,
the sigh of the brown earth beneath.

O my sad country
your soul is stained in blood.
What secrets lie buried in you weighed in tears?
The ancient slow beat within your dark-red heart,
and sky an older blue and heavily alight,
its blank bottomless sheen takes sadness' part.

O my sad country
your colours are older than story.
You have born the ravages of time and
you creak and murmur beneath the pressure of the past.
Your flat miles are millions wide
and the deep sadness is held within you fast.

O my sad country
your heart is heavy in the dry.
You have grieved for eons in the sun
mourning the future, all loves and tragedies, massacres laid bare
those spirits that hide in your caverns and wing from the mountain
   face
wailing softly the ancient pain into dusted air.

O my sad country
you ache.
You are a woman weeping for her children, their folly, their frailty,
   their fear,
your rocks and gullies, deep-blue forest, flat lands and your rivers old,
all bear witness to the passing ages, to the dreamtime murmur rising,
stories run like dark honey through your ravaged folds.

O my sad country,
you are built for sadness,
in your colour, your majesty, your mysterious form and rise,
your forest grieving, your heart mothering and ancient,
O sad country, O sad country,
drought is your blanket of sorrow, borne with dignity,
weep for the dry from your blinded ancient eyes.

On the Plains (*Drought Cycle II*)

As though the earth fights to escape itself
the outer crust cracks open
retracting. A harder denser matter emerges,
baked down to its kernel,
burnt too dry to sweat.
Apparitions of cloud to the north –
a dull brown smear –
revealed eventually as a stand of eucalypt liquefying in distance
losing their blue to the sky.
The sky relentlessly draws colour and moisture
away, as though the whole earth,
blade and tip, the barely-moist root,
each patch and scratching of colour is
evaporated.
Air like paper.
Air like burnt syrup, thickening,
and the land undulating in distance
in the same burnt-sugar shape and texture,
reduced to toffee.
The sun has no mercy, no memory of mildness.
Emus pause, expectant, flightless, gauging distance.

On the plains everything seems liquid
without one drop of water anywhere.
By the fence line, twenty miles upcountry,
a sheep kneels in supplication,
mouthing dust.
Its bones and skin are a slack grey membrane.
Mangy wool, scudding across the paddock like dirty foam,
snags on saltbush.
Crows circle.

The Big Brown (*Drought Cycle III*)

From the north-bearing train, a vision of the big brown.

The animal haunch of the hill, muscular, tensed, verging on sentience.
A land of rock and bone and sinew overlaid with balding dun-
   coloured suede.
Mile upon mile upon mile.
There is the blank submissive vulnerability, like a beaten dog.
The resignation of a landscape stripped and bowed.
The plateaux of churning-back bare hills wear their stubble nakedness
without ego or future, relinquishing all to the sky.
Further in,
intimate gullies between the brown flanks
reveal pink earth stippled with nipple-coloured stones.
The country has given itself over, shaved to the crust.
Its bareness carries majesty, and stark dignity,
like the bald head of a fasting man
incarcerated by the immensity of dry.
Mile upon mile upon mile.

The paddocks are parchment etched in haiku of stick and thistle,
grey upon grey.
Here the bleached canvas,
textured with a moulting pelt of dun velveteen,
tufts of dun grass on dun earth,
and rolling furrows of dun-coloured sheep
peeling and frothing from dry troughs
like a fount of dun-coloured sheep-textured foam.
Sparrows enunciate barrenness – sudden brown pods like a puff of
   dust.

Mile upon mile upon mile.

Even the blue hills further back have given up their blue,
dehydrated now into grey, and vaporised by the dun-coloured light.
Heat makes a boiled-sugar shimmer, and treelines liquefy in distance.
Western New South Wales is dying of thirst, burning alive,
parched, panting and melted to bone.
It is the big brown.
It is the big big dry.

Skeletons of sheep, galah and kangaroo punctuate the parchment space,
Interspersed with saltbush, white lichen on bleached rock, and
    thistles dried to sculptural white.
The big brown is adorned by these installations of the artful dry.
Dead stands of eucalypt capitulate,
and collapse themselves into symmetries of silent grace.
All is made of the beautiful dead bones.
The whole world is a sun-dried skeleton.
And the sky is as big as grief, so very pale, empty and massive,
until it becomes an infinite absence.

This drought is the magnificent absence,
and the continent groans and sags beneath its empty weight.

*

From the wrinkle of the ranges, the big brown seeps inland,
condensed by the fierce and waterless sky
into a red centre.
Rain is a memory of some other dream, and
the continent soaks instead in light,
awash with the blinding white and high.

Like skin calloused, hard-used and aching for moisture,
the earth, dried and cracked, splits,
but no blood comes, as it has dried too.
The internal juice of the earth has dried and retreated.
Crows sing the song of the big brown
Ark! Ark! Ahhhhhhrrrk…the downward slope of the last,
to a final pitiless nonchalance.
Into the pit of a dam, concentric tiers, as though
fashioned on a great potter's wheel, down and round and down and round,
to a bottom made of tessellated mud, caking, splitting.
In the hint of moisture there, yabbies reach in clawed
desperation, glued to the earth by useless mud, and the carcass of a calf
who trembled down to drink, whom the earth clamped, who could not ascend.

*

The land holds fast,
eternal, unmovable and resilient.
Any rain that once fell was the promise of a different future.

*

Further on northern greens will appear suddenly,
the obscene indulgence of bobbing laden trees,
stands of grasses in their crass green…
I no longer believe in them.

The big brown has become my familiar,
these years of dry, the slow bake:
my country, waterless and sheer.
In my heart I return to the frank humility of
land and sky awaiting colour
bowing to the hand of a dry god.

Bushfire (*Drought Cycle IV*)

A million hectares razed
and the mountain and our secret lake
enveloped with unholy blaze.
Invisible –
the air was thick with smoke,
pressing in like fog,
claustrophobia ensued.
I could not breathe
thinking of you.
And drove as if I were blind
and the world was blind
and I was in a nightmare
made of smoke.
I could not find the way.
The mountain burned
and burned
and the smoke
tore our eyes and
we were lost.
I ran out into it, needing air
but there was none.
Choking, I returned and
found my breath was gone
though I would give it all to you
to breathe you back to life.
Drought can cause the hardiest to falter,
and the smoke fills every crevice
with the scent of hell.

Communion: The Dreaming Tree

The Kalari people identified this canoe tree as a spiritual totem to be preserved. It stands preserved in the middle of a crop paddock bearing the incision where materials for the bark canoe were removed.

Communion I

Through the sea paddock I travel,
a sailor of grasses, the black cattle magic fish
in the rustling dust of my wake.
Old bull leviathan drags his scrotum like a
bulging trawler's net,
nudges himself against heifers' soft flanks
like a berthing liner. Contemplative in his
immense carnality, he is an enlightened gargantuan buddha.

It seems the world is rushing to a falling sun.
I push against the tide and currents of warm air
surge back. Insects are minnow pods, churning,
as I ride the gauntlet of barley oceans,
the nascent heads a foam of blue.
Colours run to the horizon where an intensity
Of light bespeaks God.
The miles of flat land subside – a bay at low tide –
And red gums groan as their blood cools,
octopus-twisted and fleshy.
Silhouetted fence lines are netting and buoys, and
the rustling sea paddock turns powdered lavender,
tidal flats of parched furrows
expose the magnitude of drought.

Rising from the blue barley, the dreaming tree,
my sweet Atlantis,
is awaiting me.

*

Here at the edge and heart of the world
the profound composure of the devout encloses me
like a wing…
while all the world slows…
and stops…

the silence is a
Holy magnificence.

Communion II (Yellowbox Country)

'Yellowbox means good country,' he said,
and the country was full of yellowbox.

The colour of sap ran over the country
and shone against trees high up.
The yellowbox was the biggest tree, alone in the paddock,
divined all colour and energy and shed them skyward.
Honeybox.
Melliodora.
Tree of the flying canoe, of the dreaming,
risen from blood-coloured land.
Blood tree.
Heart tree.

*

Yellowbox means good cooking, burns
in the wood stove steady, deep and hot.
This one not for burning.

Pressed against the trunk, look up,
take in the wooded smell, sap-flavoured light
refracted off fertile flooded soil of that red country…
and the bark like burnt sugared pastry,
bark like cinnamon sticks,
like bush damper cooked in blood and honey,
in the blood and honey land.

*

Straight up from the base
the sweet dreaming tree spreads across the sky,
spilling her sugared beauty down.
Her spirit radiating.

Skyward, the impression of clouds of bees –
lemony things fine and filigree limey light fingered and shushing
beautiful hazy dusty polleny, powdery floating cloudiness,
blossom-promise, buds that flicker through lime-juice light
and send a rosy glow to quench the reticent air.
A sense of clustered jewels shimmering in heights.
Shedding feathery sugar upon glistening air,
a sense of green glomesh.

'Notice,' says the elder, pointing up along the crown,
'how the branches come off the tree differently higher up and across.'
Notice the detail, its division and its unhurried repetition of
internal form, the essence of the understanding of the tree.
The shape of her branches and turnings, the direction of her
expression of herself, her will to convey herself.
This is different to trees in other country –

*

Induced, the pretty-faced calves gather, black, doe-eyed and blinking,
to stamp and blow a little, and gather their bovine flanks
into a sacred circle, about the tree,
make a music of their quiet butting, chewing, and noisy streams of piss
strong with the river grass pungency.
Snort and stamp and shine with steam
in that profoundly clear winter light.

and the sound of the high breezes quickening,
the rising and murmuring and chiming,
billowed then dying, stirring the syruplight-
underground and from the beams of sun and out of the knots of tree.
like a dark harp, the hushed breath of the tree's own heart.

*

The land is vast
And beyond ancient.
The yellowbox tree says this.

*

I lay my head down,
and the beat of heart matched the beat
from the heart of the earth, that rose
through the dreaming tree…

Coda

The paddock a pitching of waters in the heliotrope light,
forest looming like a pod of whales to the east,
and the sky as mysterious and deep as ocean.
Black cattle like great sleek fish cruise and hover within
the dark netting of night, clustering.
The tree releases me into the darkening murmur of evening,
and I steer forward, mariner in a small boat with a heart
weighted like burning stone, hoping for safe passage
through the perils of night
to the one light burning there on the distant shore.
Compassless in the storm
save the tree,
the spirit epiphany.

Prehistorica *Birds and Dogs*

Birds sit still and tucked in the dark.
Flutter-bunches of finches in the mulga; crotchets and quavers of cockatoos;
and humped galahs, astring in the wastrel tops of the gums;
hens in the chook-house, plumped like small pillows, roosting, ruffling and snuffling down;
plovers frumping in the grass clumps;
magpies, butcher birds, once freewheeling clerks and strutting solicitors, transformed to dark smudges in trees;
and ruffian crows and villain choughs and quincy rosellas like harlequin puppets strung in branches,
in the gums and the melaleuca, and peewees and willy wagtails tiny commas and signatures on the night's scroll;
and kookaburras, sharp-shafted noble-turquoise, half-beak/half-body,
tucked big heads into gobbling wings on the white gums and paperbarks.
In shaggy peppercorn outlines of dishevelment – and fig and mulberry
in the gardens and yards and along lanes and fence lines.
Nuzzling grass parrots clustered like feijoas, like fruit in hollows
and swallows festooning the old lady she-oaks and paper hawks in tussocks
and falcons in silky oaks and minors in willows, a silenced ornithological cacophony.
Birds birds, shivery strings of day birds stilled, hung amongst the night,
bedded down, roosting and nesting and perching and clinging.
And even the nocturnes rest, tawny frog-mouth and hoot owls tired
from winging and tearing field mice and dropping from darkness like stealthy scimitars, sit staring surprised and utter.

All silent, flattened and still.
No bird sound in that godless lunar time,
three a.m, beyond day.

Stealthily does light emerge from somewhere nearer four,
a ghost of day, lurking hint, not quite believed.
For birds, and dogs, in the farmyard four a.m begins with an evanescence, a bare irradiation,
wheedling them from sleep, an irritant, probing their unhuman dreams.
Their eyes as ancient as rock, matt and beaded like quartz,
some less intelligence, reined to a deeper rhythm down in the primitive bedrock,
brown pebbles with slits, flutter slightly at the barest shift from utter dark to the barest, barest film of promised light.
The vague expectancy, the cold like stone
and the air is swept by the bitter pre-dawn cooling.
Was it never light before this?

And yet, and yet, the flesh of dogs and birds, their guts and wings, infuse with the thought of that impossible light,
as though the first to come upon the world.
Those creatures feel the light before light,
that smear of opalescence proffered with a thumbnail at the coalition of the earth and sky.

A false start, and dogs groan and rattle at chain restlessly, dog-guttural, dingo-dogged,
sniffing, licking each other and scratching absently, the underbelly,
convulsive scratching, licking the quivering pink, wet-nosed scruffy tumescence, dirty dogginess, dust-ridden,
twitching at the tick of impending daylight, the turbid unclear pre-dawn blindness.
The whole yard and the trees and paddocks begin to twitch, peck and scratch.
Around the house they wait expectant, for that sunrise, that will sweep up all in its flooding path,
and flatten the day with its heat, the tidal wave of light.

Later, dogs will lie in shade pools, pressed to the earth,
and birds stranded on lawn, will pant,
in inhuman heat, without complaint.

Convincing Ground

The country cannot hide
its winter beauty
the moody shining ground:
there is the mantle of dew
crystal netting hung on paddocks of etched blades –
a foreground of glitter, silver and clean
a feeling of knives and diamond,
of satiate lurex and blinding hematite,
something inscrutable
there is the sky way back
piled to the treeline with grey cloud
a sense of snow, ermine collar
gathered to the shoulder of the forest
there is the white-gold medallion of sun
patrician through moveless leaves
the air's ice-water splash
clearer than glass
and the soil tooled in whorled shapes, like worked teak,
black as cacao, rich as cake
black earth ripe for the seed
there is completed stillness
there is mist like remnants of hurried breath
there is the river's frozen honey
the forest stately and remote, exudes
the scents of dark, the vaults of dark colour,
shadows and ice and glistening gunmetal tears
wet and shining in winter.

The Divine Mundane

At school in the morning

rows of little feet, all decked out
in matching socks and polished matching shoes,
and hair all brushed and braided…
the hours of toil, the scatter and the scurry,
the calling and pulling hidden there in that
small order…
ordinary miracles of daily life.

www.ingramcontent.com/pod-product-compliance
Lightning Source LLC
Chambersburg PA
CBHW070051120526
44589CB00034B/1935